Devil Cat

Adrian Keefe

HODDER &
STOUGHTON

First published in Great Britain in 2006

The right of Adrian Keefe to be identified as the Author of the Work has been asserted by him
in accordance with the Copyright, Designs and Patents Act 1988.

2

British Library Cataloguing in Publication Data
A record for this book is available from the British Library

ISBN – 10: 0 340 908769
ISBN – 13: 978 0340 908761

Printed and bound in Great Britain by
CPI Bath

The paper used in this hardback is a natural recyclable product made
from wood grown in sustainable forests. The hard cover board is recycled.

Hodder & Stoughton
A Division of Hodder Headline Ltd
338 Euston Road
London NW1 3BH
www.madaboutbooks.com

For Barry & Terry

Special thanks to Neil

Thanks to Abbie, Stan, Tony Bunton, Stephen Orr,
Darren Horder, Jim Edgar, the Mitchell Library, Kallkwik in Glasgow,
the GFT, cats & cat lovers everywhere

This book belongs to... (your stupid name here)

Thank you for buying or accepting my book as a gift. Thank you for being a dotty 'cat person'. Thank you for not having enough romance in your life and deluding yourself that there is a symbiotic, loving relationship between you and your cat(s). Thank you for feeding us too much rich food, providing us with warm, secure homes, paying our medical bills, allowing us to lead a life of luxurious leisure, stroking us and especially for giving us access to your frequently sofa-bound, squidgy thighs. In short, thanks for being a sucker. We could live in the wild, but we know a cushy number when we see one.

'But Snuggles loves me', I hear you whine. Yeah, sure he loves you. He doesn't even want to know you after he's been fed, but sure, he loves you.

It's not your fault you're a pathetic human and lead a pitiful ant-like existence. You have an inner directive telling you to be busy, to do things for other people, to spend a lot of your time engaging in activities you don't enjoy. It's not our fault we lead selfish lives. We have an inner directive telling us: 'eat until your belly is full, sleep until your belly is empty, eat until your belly is full, sleep …'

My real name is Devil Cat, although I humour my dippy human servant, Suzy, by letting her call me Sooty. I am the Spawn of Satan. God's son was human. My old man chose cats to bring his beliefs into the world. Go figure. It's not that cats are evil, it's just that we are proud, greedy, lustful, envious, gluttonous, angry and slothful; we kill, steal, commit adultery and not only covet our neighbour's house, but defile his flowerbeds.

I live in the small village of Blackness in West Lothian, near Edinburgh. The Castle of Blackness is my ancestral home, although I've shacked up with a blonde in a small maisonette, as castles are very draughty places. Her personality and intelligence are somewhat lacking and yet she attends to my every need and goes out to work, so I get the place to myself a lot. I just wish that she'd accept being a sad old spinster and realise she was put on this Earth to look after me. She goes out with loads of men, but relationships elude her. She should give up the dating scene and surrender her warm, sweetly-scented, badly-toned body to me.

Finally, hell forbid; if you are a non-believer and don't worship us felines; be careful if you mistreat one of us, because he just may well be the Pussy of Pandemonium, Kitten of Cabbala, Animal Antichrist, Devil Cat, ha, ha, ha…

Favourites

	Devil Cat	Suzy
Ideal partner	A very young Siamese or a fat old woman	George Clooney (swoon!)
TV	Cat food ads	Sex & the City
Film	Eraserhead	Sleepless in Seattle
Author	Machiavelli	Marian Keyes
Painter	Rothko	Jack Vettriano
Music	Birdsong at close quarters	Westlife (swoon!)
Sport	Late-night poker	Jazzercise
Food	King prawns fried in butter dipped in whipped cream at room temperature	Dairy Milk
Drink	The above liquidised	Diet Coke
Colour	Black with a hint of jet	Baby pink
Time of day	Half-past bedtime	Elevenses
Time of year	Bleak mid-winter (in front of a roaring fire)	Early spring
Body part	The hand that feeds me	George Clooney's bottom!
Smell	Fear	New-born babies
Country	The Land of Nod	Tenerife

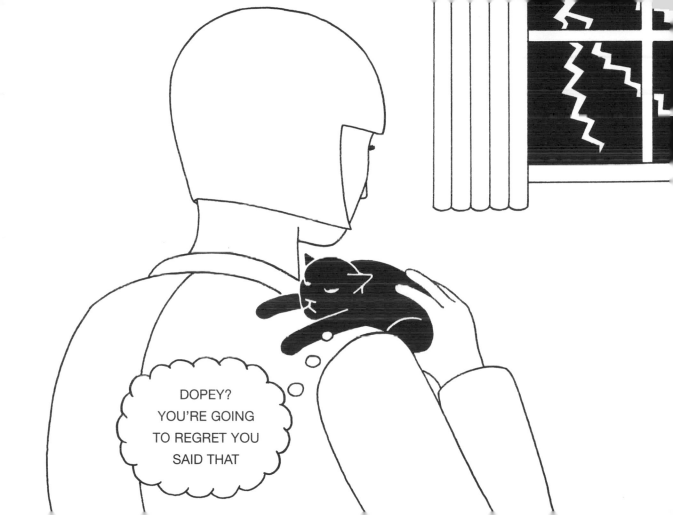

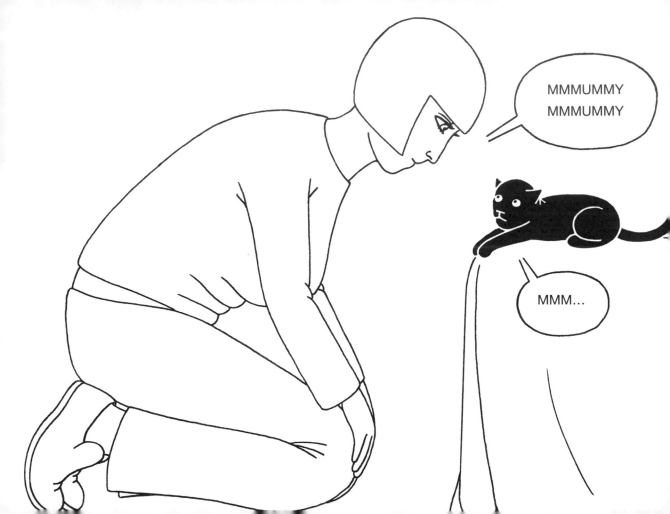

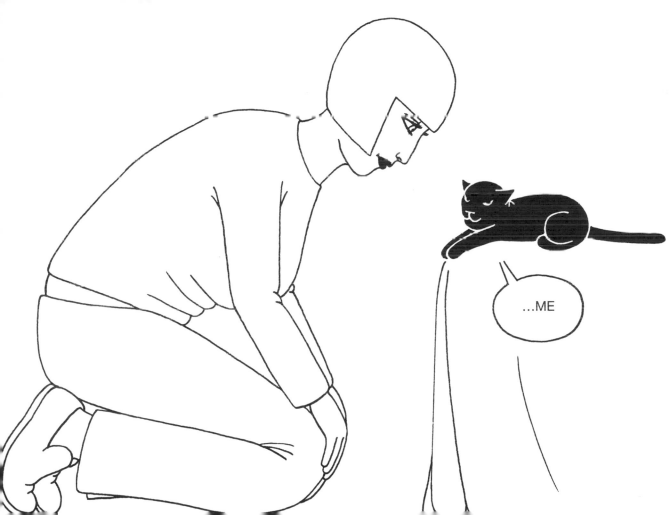

INDOOR FELINE PERSONALITY

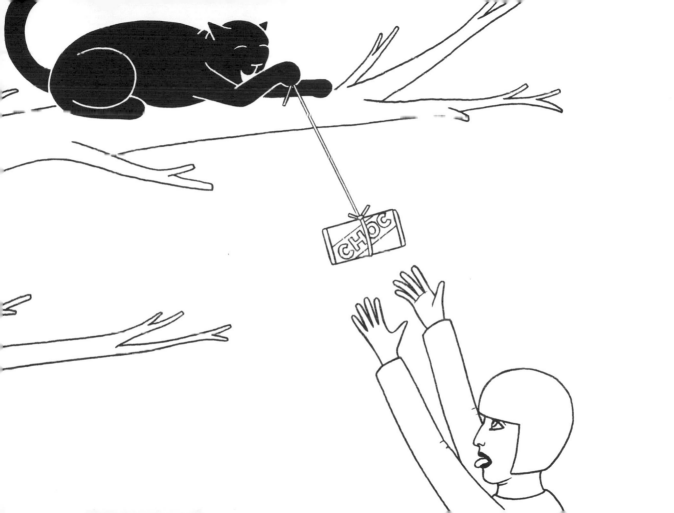

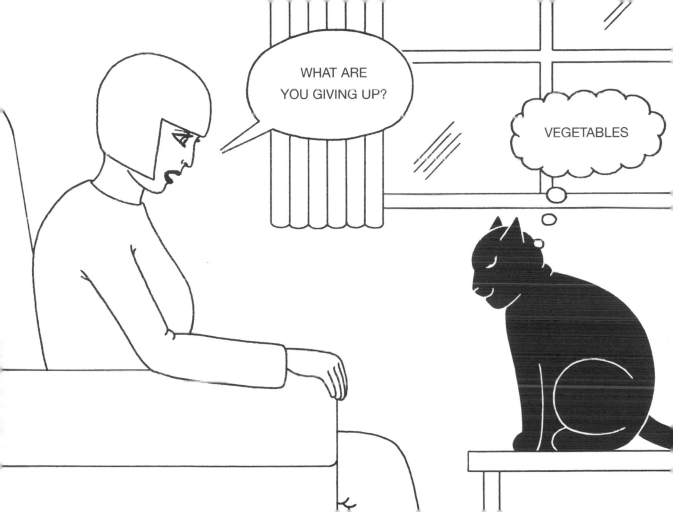

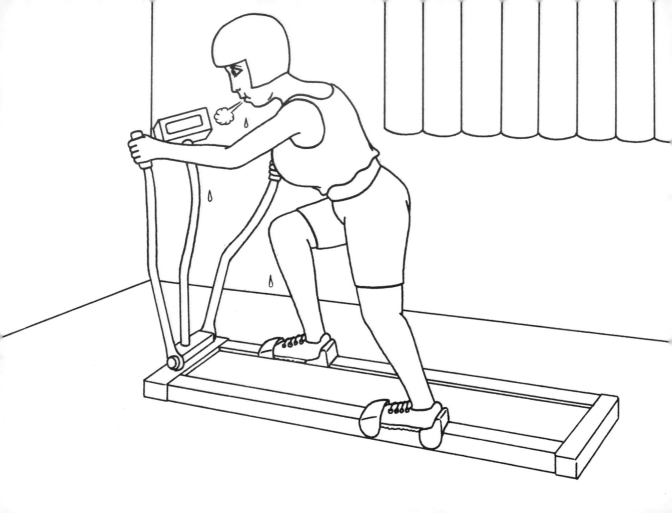

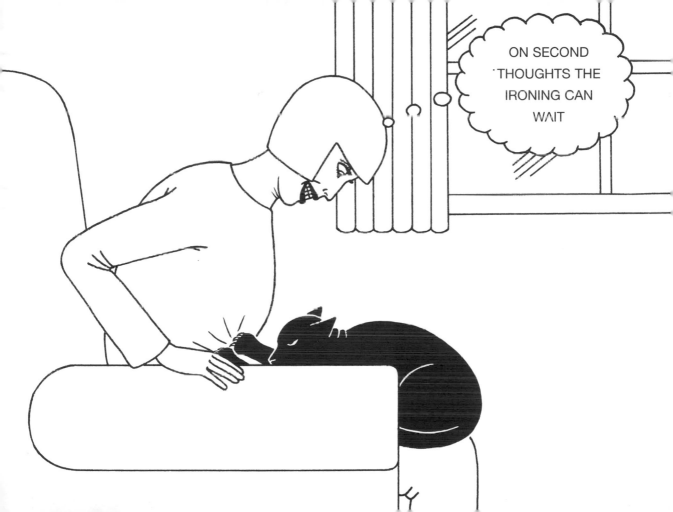

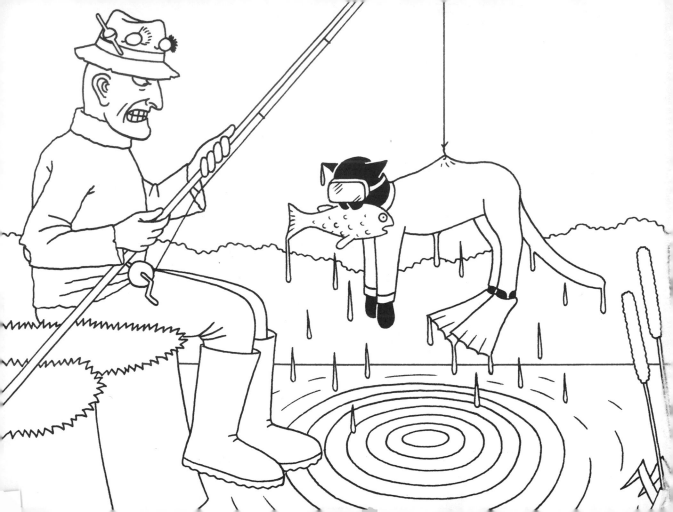